J $9.95
567.9   Dixon, Dougal
Di   The very first
            dinosaurs

DATE DUE

MR 21 '9	JAN 7 2	NO 15 '79
AG 28 '91	FE 08 2	JN 22 '23
JA 21 9	OCT 17 9	
JE 19 '0	JAN 22 9	
SE 28 '92	MY 16 9	
JE 10 '93	JUL 09 9	
AG 3 '93	SEP 22 7	
MAR 8 '9	MR 17 00	
JUL 8 '0	MY 17 '00	
AUG 11 9	MR 01 94	
FE 8 '0	AG 07 10	
OCT 20 '94	NO 16 '10	

DEMCO

The Very First
DINOSAURS

**For a free color catalog describing Gareth Stevens' list
of high-quality children's books call 1-800-341-3569**

Library of Congress Cataloging-in-Publication Data

Dixon, Dougal.
   [First dinosaurs]
     The very first dinosaurs / text by Dougal Dixon; photography by Jane Burton;
artwork of photographed reptiles by Steve Kirk. -- US ed.
       p. cm. -- (My first dinosaur library)
     First conceived as The first dinosaurs; based on The age of dinosaurs by Jane Burton and
Dougal Dixon.
     Summary: Brief text and pictures introduce thirteen dinosaurs, providing information on
appearance, habitat, and eating habits.
     ISBN 0-8368-0151-2
     1. Dinosaurs--Juvenile literature. [1. Dinosaurs.] I. Burton, Jane, ill. II. Kirk, Steve,
ill. III. Title. IV. Series: Dixon, Dougal. My first dinosaur library.
QE862.D5D537   1989
567.9'1--dc20   89-11336

This North American edition first published in 1989 by
Gareth Stevens Children's Books
RiverCenter Building, Suite 201
1555 North RiverCenter Drive
Milwaukee, Wisconsin 53212, USA

This US edition copyright © 1989. Adapted from *The First Dinosaurs*, which was
based on *The Age of Dinosaurs*, by Jane Burton and Dougal Dixon. Conceived and
produced by Eddison/Sadd Editions, London. First published in the United Kingdom
and Australia by Sphere Books, London, 1984, and in the United States under the title
Time Exposure, by Beaufort Books, New York, 1984.

Series Editor: Valerie Weber
Editor: Julie Brown

Printed in the United States of America

1 2 3 4 5 6 7 8 9 96 95 94 93 92 91 90 89

The Very First
DINOSAURS

Photography by
Jane Burton

Text by
Dougal Dixon

Artwork of Photographed Reptiles by
Steve Kirk

Gareth Stevens Children's Books
MILWAUKEE

Learning about the
DINOSAURS

The Very First
DINOSAURS

When
DINOSAURS
Ruled the Earth

The Last of the
DINOSAURS

The Very First Dinosaurs

About 345 million years ago, reptiles appeared on Earth. Their descendants were the dinosaurs. They appeared about 225 million years ago. They shared the Earth with other reptiles.

This book is about some of the animals that lived during the first part of the Age of Dinosaurs. It lasted 35 million years.

CONTENTS

Note to the reader: While you are reading this book, you will find certain words appearing in **bold type**. This means the word is listed in the "New Words" section on page 31.

HYLONOMUS

Hylonomus was one of the first **reptiles**. Like today's lizards, it had dry skin.

Hylonomus laid its leathery eggs on land. A baby Hylonomus looked just like an adult, only smaller.

How to say its name: **hi-LON-oh-muss**
Length: 3 feet (1 meter)
Food: insects
Found in Nova Scotia

Its skeleton looked like the skeleton of today's lizards.

Like Dimetrodon,
Edaphosaurus had a fin.
These dinosaurs were also
about the same size.
Edaphosaurus ate plants.

DIMETRODON

Dimetrodon had a fin on its back. It looked like a sail. This fin could **absorb** the Sun's rays to keep Dimetrodon warm.

Dimetrodon had long front teeth for catching its **prey**.

How to say its name: **die-MET-ruh-don**
Length: 11 feet (3 meters)
Food: meat
Found in Texas and Oklahoma

LYCAENOPS

Lycaenops had long legs. They lifted its body straight up off the ground. It looked like today's dog and could run quickly.

Lycaenops was active and strong. It had long, sharp teeth for killing its prey.

How to say its name: **lie-KAY-nops**
Length: 3 feet (1 meter)
Food: meat
Found in South Africa

Lycaenops (1) stood on
straight legs. Pareiasaurus
(2) had legs that sprawled
sideways.

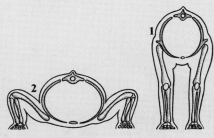

This is a skeleton of Cynognathus. It looks
like the skeleton of a dog.

CYNOGNATHUS

In many ways, Cynognathus looked like today's **mammals**. It had hair and whiskers. It was probably **warm-blooded**.

But Cynognathus was still a reptile. It had a large jaw and probably laid eggs. The mother may have nursed her babies.

How to say its name: **sy-nog-NAY-thus**
Length: 6 feet (2 meters)
Food: meat
Found in South Africa

LYSTROSAURUS

Lystrosaurus lived in the water. Its nose and eyes were on top of its head. It could stay under water but keep its eyes above water.

It looked clumsy but could swim well. It could also walk on land.

How to say its name: **liss-troh-SAW-rus**
Length: 3 feet (1 meter)
Food: water plants
Found in South Africa, India, and Antarctica

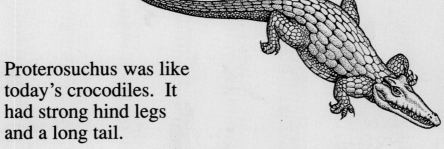

Proterosuchus was like
today's crocodiles. It
had strong hind legs
and a long tail.

PROTEROSUCHUS

Proterosuchus lived in the water like Lystrosaurus. It could swim easily with its long body and flat tail.

Its long jaws were like a trap for catching fish.

How to say its name: **pro-tair-oh-SOOK-us**
Length: 5 feet (1.5 meters)
Food: fish, other water animals
Found in Africa

PODOPTERYX and LONGISQUAMA

Podopteryx looked like a small lizard. It had a special web of skin between its legs. This helped it fly like a glider.

Longisquama had a **crest** of long scales. These were probably an early form of feathers.

Podopteryx
How to say its name: **po-DOP-ter-ix**
Length: 1 foot (30 centimeters)
Food: meat   Found in the USSR

Longisquama
How to say its name: **long-iss-KWAH-ma**
Length: 6 inches (15 centimeters)
Food: meat   Found in the USSR

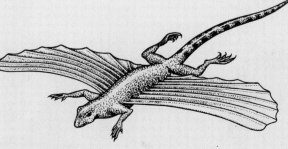

Kuehneosaurus
could fly. Its ribs
supported its wings.

19

These skeletons
are of an adult
Nothosaurus and
two babies.

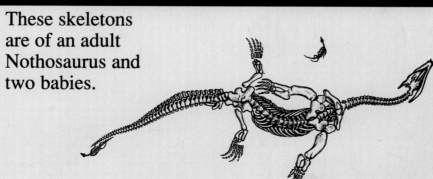

NOTHOSAURUS and TANYSTROPHEUS

Nothosaurus was a swimming reptile. It used its feet as paddles and its tail as a fin.

Tanystropheus had a neck that would have reached from the ground to a basketball hoop! This long neck helped it reach fish in pools of water.

Nothosaurus
How to say its name: **no-THO-saw-rus**
Length: 10 feet (3 meters)   Food: fish
Found in England, Israel, Jordan, India, and China

Tanystropheus
How to say its name: **tan-ees-TRO-fee-us**
Length: 13 feet (4 meters)   Food: fish
Found in Poland

SALTOPUS

Saltopus was a tiny dinosaur built like a chicken. It walked on its hind feet. It used its hands to catch prey. Each hand had five fingers.

Morganucodon was one of the earliest mammals. It was also a favorite Saltopus meal.

How to say its name: **SALT-oh-pus**
Length: 2 feet (60 centimeters)
Food: meat
Found in Scotland

People once thought these
Saltopus tracks were bird
tracks that became **fossils**.

This is a Hyperodapedon
skull. It shows that the
upper jaw had two rows
of teeth on each side.

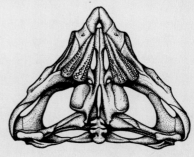

HYPERODAPEDON

Hyperodapedon had a beak to nip off soft plants. It used its back teeth like scissors to chop its meal.

Plant life changed over the years from soft plants to trees. So Hyperodapedon may have died out because it no longer had soft plants to eat.

How to say its name: **hi-pare-oh-DAP-ih-don**
Length: 4 feet (1 meter)
Food: plants
Found in Scotland

THECODONTOSAURUS

Thecodontosaurus traveled in **herds**. The herds lived in the hills during the rainy season. They **migrated** to the plains when the weather was warm and dry.

Thecodontosaurus ate both plants and animals. It could walk on its back legs or on all four legs.

How to say its name: **thee-kuh-DON-tuh-saw-rus**
Length: 6 feet (2 meters)
Food: plants and animals
Found in England and South Africa

Thecodontosaurus (2) was
related to both meat-eaters (1)
and plant-eaters (3).

Fun Facts about Dinosaur and Animal Life

1.   Starfish, clams, ants, and cockroaches lived with these ancient dinosaurs. They still survive today.

2.   We cannot know what color the dinosaurs were. Their color probably depended on where they lived. Plus, male and female dinosaurs were probably different colors.

3.   Dinosaurs laid eggs. But people have found large fossils of some newly born dinosaurs. This puzzles scientists. They wonder if dinosaurs might have given birth to live young.

4.   Some plant-eating dinosaurs had several rows of teeth — often up to 2,000 teeth in their mouth at one time!

5.   When the first dinosaurs lived, all the continents were pushed into one large land mass. Scientists named it "Pangaea." This term means "all earth."

6. Meat-eating dinosaurs probably ran very fast to catch prey. Or maybe they were strong and had sharp claws.

7. Crocodiles came from thecodonts. These reptiles lived 200 million years ago.

8. Feathers are a type of scale. They probably developed to keep animals warm.

9. Some dinosaurs swallowed stones to help grind their food. Today's crocodiles and birds swallow stones for the same purpose.

10. The jellyfish was one of the first animals that had a mouth and a stomach.

11. Coelophysis is the oldest well known dinosaur. Scientists think that it may have been a cannibal and eaten others of its kind. Fossils have been found with other small Coelophysis bones inside.

More Books about Dinosaurs

Here are more books about dinosaurs and other animals of their time.

The First Days of the Dinosaurs.
    Gabriele (Penny Lane)
How Dinosaurs Lived.
    Benton (Franklin Watts)
More about Dinosaurs.
    Cutts (Troll)
My Visit to the Dinosaurs.
    Aliki (Harper & Row)
Prehistoric Monsters.
    Brasch (Salem House)

New Words

absorb ....to take in or soak up
something.

crest ....a bony or hairy growth on an
animal.

fossils ....remains of plants or animals
preserved in rocks.

herd ....a group of animals living
together.

mammals ....animals that give birth to live
young and that are warm-
blooded. They often have fur
or hairy skin.

migrated......................moved from one area to
another.

prey ....an animal killed for food.

reptiles ....cold-blooded animals that lay
eggs on dry ground. Reptiles
have horny skin or scales.

warm-blooded................able to control body
temperature.

Index and Pronunciation Guide